TOP TENS

Terrific Tips on Friends, Family, Happiness & More!

by Lia Haberman

SCHOLASTIC INC.
New York Toronto London Auckland Sydney
Mexico City New Delhi Hong Kong

ISBN 0-439-14028-5

12 11 10 9 8 7 6 5 4 3 2 1   9/9 01 2 3 4/0

Printed in the U.S.A.

First Scholastic printing, November 1999

Contents

Introduction
All About Top Tens

This book brings together the best tips ever collected for *All About You* magazine. Each chapter offers lists with ten tips each on topics such as surviving your siblings, having fun even when your friends aren't around, talking to boys without breaking into a sweat, giving your bedroom a supercheap makeover, and making the world a better place! These top ten lists are meant to answer as many questions about friends, family, school, boys, beauty, and health as possible.

Of course, just because we at *All About You* magazine like to give advice doesn't mean we're necessarily very good at following it.

We all still have bad hair days and wardrobe dilemmas. We fight with our friends and our parents. We get tongue-tied when we run into cute guys in the office. Being a college graduate definitely doesn't make you supersuave!

But during our research for the magazine stories, we talk to counselors, social workers, therapists, and hairstylists all the time — and we always learn something new. These people are experts at giving advice. Their knowledge can make us a little bit smarter, healthier, and happier — and we've included their advice here. This is the wisdom *All About You* has to offer and we want to share it with you, from the very serious to the downright silly. We hope this book will help make your life a little easier and a lot more fun.

Chapter One
Girlfriends and Boys

Girlfriends: Getting to Know Her

Got a new friend you'd like to know better but don't know how to get closer? Or maybe you're just feeling out of touch with an old pal and want to regain contact. Don't worry, getting to know her better is easier than you might think once you make the commitment to opening up and sharing.

1. It's a snap. Ever look at your friend's photo albums? If you take the time to find out who's who in her family tree, you'll get to know more about her (she's got her aunt Edna's big ears, for example) and that could bring you closer together.

3

2. A few of her favorite things. What makes your friend tick? What puts a smile on her face and a spring in her step? This need-to-know info will come in handy the next time she's feeling down. So pay attention when she raves about her favorite movie or the yummy Hawaiian pizza she ate last night.

3. Now you know. Everyone's got something that makes them special. Maybe your friend makes the best brownies, speaks another language, or writes travel diaries every time she takes a family trip. Show some interest in her hobbies. You could ask if she'll share her brownie recipe — it'll be a bonding experience and she'll appreciate the attention. And who knows, you might even develop a new interest.

4. Family friend. Your friend probably doesn't base her opinion of you on what her parents think of you, but if her folks don't care for you it could definitely affect how much you'll get to hang with her. So whenever you're invited over and her parents are around, be on your best behavior. Make small talk and always be friendly to them, even if your friend is scowling at them; *don't* treat your friends' parents like they are the enemy! The more her parents like you, the more likely you'll receive another invite to her house — and a chance to get even closer to your friend.

5. Get involved. Find out what after-school activities your friend is involved in and if it's something that interests you, consider signing up. Sharing a hobby will definitely bring the two of you closer together.

6. Her friends are your friends. You picked your friend because she seemed like an amazing person, right? Others have probably noticed her good qualities, too. So don't get bummed out if she has lots of other friends, too — it just means you've got good taste. Besides, if you spend some time getting to know her other pals, you'll score points for not playing the possessive-friend game.

7. Listen up. Being a good friend means being a great listener. That doesn't mean you have to come up with expert advice all the time — on the contrary, it's your silence that's valued. Your bud'll come to you when she's got something on her mind if she feels you are there to hear her out — she'll know that you really care.

8. **Famous faces.** Ask your friend if she could be anyone for a day, who would she be? You could learn a lot about your *amiga* by discovering whether she aspires to achieve glamour-girl status or would prefer to be a savvy businesswoman. Who she sees herself becoming in the future definitely has to do with what she thinks of herself in the present.

9. **Bonding time.** Nothing will bring the two of you closer than a shared experience. So get off the couch (unless bonding over daytime TV is your idea of fun) and invite your friend out for the afternoon. You don't have to do anything crazy — just doing stuff together will bring you closer.

10. **Fill in the blank.** Want to jump-start the getting-to-know-you phase? Take turns making the following statement: "One thing you don't know about me is . . ." You and your friend-to-be will learn a lot more about each other.

Friendship Failure

You spend years sharing everything, then all of a sudden you can't find a thing to say to the girl you thought was your B.F. for life. Check out the following signs of a failing friendship. If a bunch of these signs sound familiar, you have a choice: Roll up your sleeves and work at this relationship or cut your losses before anyone gets really hurt.

1. Self-esteem SOS. She used to make you laugh, but now she just seems to be laughing *at* you all the time and your self-esteem is taking a serious nosedive. You don't need that.

2. The truth is tricky. Whether you're telling giant fibs or little white lies, if neither of you is telling the truth to each other, that's a big problem.

3. Memories. You spend more time thinking back on the good old days than hav-

ing fun times together in the present —
maybe it's over.

4. Behind her back. You're secretly complaining to your other friends about her flaws.
If you don't appreciate her one hundred
percent for who she is, then you just don't appreciate her. And *she* deserves better than
that.

5. Hush up. Neither of you feels like you
can be open and honest with each other
about what's going on. Long-lasting, real
friendships are based on openness and hon-
esty — if you don't have this, forget it.

6. Feeling blue. The whole friendship is
basically bringing you down and affecting
every aspect of your life. Friends should lift
you up, not drag you down.

7. Going nuts. She's always cracked her
knuckles and it never bothered you before
but now everything she does drives you up a
wall. Sounds like it's time to take a break from
each other.

8. **Busted.** You've learned all about her back-stabbing ways and now you don't think you can ever trust her again. Trust is key — without it you can't have a friendship.

9. **Busy, busy, busy.** You're constantly finding yourself making excuses so you won't have to spend as much time with her, even though it's putting a serious damper on your social life. Stop hiding away and face the music.

10. **Low on the list.** Fixing the friendship is not high on your list of priorities. In fact, you pretty much couldn't care less if the two of you patch up your differences. Obviously, you are ready to move on.

Be a Great Friend

You don't have to be the princess of popularity to be happy but you do need some good friends who will stick with you through thick and thin. Most of the time things will probably take care of themselves — you'll be surrounded by great pals who are nice and supportive of you. But every once in a while you'll have to make the extra effort to guarantee long-lasting friendship.

1. Say you're sorry. If you messed up, admit you acted like a jerk and apologize. You might think sending her a belated birthday card is no big deal but maybe it really bothers her when you forget about her big day. Put yourself in her shoes — how would it make you feel? Exactly . . . so say you're sorry already!

2. Friends and boys don't mix. Never fall for her crush or visit her house just to see her cute older brother. If she finds out you like her crush, she may lose all trust in you (after all, *she* liked him *first*). And if she catches on that you're into her brother more than you are into her, well, she just might decide that's why you are friends with her — to get to him. Either situation spells really bad news for your friendship.

3. Her friends are your friends. You think your friend is a wonderful person, right? Well, so do other people. Don't act possessive or else you might drive her away to a more accepting circle of friends.

4. Be a good listener. If she needs to talk, don't be judgmental or overtake the conversation with your own stories. Feel flattered that she chose you to confide in — listen, be supportive, and offer advice if she asks for it.

5. Don't go green with envy. Everyone does something well. Don't envy the talents she possesses, whether it's the ability to ace math tests or throw together the perfect outfit. Those are the things she does well (and probably that you admire) and you should feel happy for her — you have your own talents, after all.

6. Keep quiet. Never blab a secret she's told you, unless it's so terrible you'd be saving her life to tell someone — spreading the news of her latest crush doesn't count.

7. Never forget. You need the memory of an elephant to be a good friend. People feel really special when you remember small random details about them most others would never recall — it shows you are paying attention to what she talks about and that you think she's important. And *never ever* forget her birthday!

8. **Stick up for each other.** If someone at school is making fun of your friend, it's your job to defend her — even if it doesn't win you any popularity contests.

9. **Give her some space.** Even the best of friends can get on each other's nerves. Don't panic that this signals the end of your friendship — you probably just need a little space in order to appreciate each other all over again.

10. **Don't be a fair-weather friend.** Don't turn your back on a friend who's going through a difficult phase — that's when she needs you the most. When something goes wrong and you're feeling blue, don't call her only because she's a good listener. Be there for the good and the bad.

Be the Perfect Dinner Guest (or How to Make Sure Your Friend's Parents Will Invite You Back)

So, who needs tips on eating at a friend's house, you might ask? Like, how difficult is it to get the fork to your mouth? Well, if you're hoping to be invited back, it might not be a bad idea to brush up on your dinner-table etiquette: Elbows off the table, chew with your mouth shut, and smile, even if you're being served brussels sprouts.

1. **The real deal.** If you're a vegetarian you don't have to be shy about it — tell your friend's parents. They don't have to go out of their way for you but at least then they'll know not to serve you a meat loaf.

2. **Veggie by choice.** While stating your preference for vegetarian food is fine, don't force your lifestyle on everyone else. Boasting to your host, "I don't eat food with a face," and making everyone else feel like a barbarian is just plain rude.

3. **Meet and greet.** If you're having dinner with your friend's parents for the first time, make sure you introduce yourself and shake hands before dinner starts.

4. Set up. Even if your friend thinks helping her folks is bogus, offer to set the table, serve drinks, or do anything else that could help out. Your friend might accuse you of being a brownnose but she'd probably do the same thing at your house and her parents will certainly appreciate it!

5. Chitchat. Don't just gobble your meal and run. Act interested by making small talk: Ask about a recent vacation the family has taken or an activity you know they enjoy doing together. It's polite.

6. Finger free. Even if you eat with your fingers at home, always use a knife and fork when you're a guest. But don't clutch the cutlery while you eat — place it on the side of the plate while you're chewing. Of course, if your hosts eat with their fingers (like if you're having pizza or sandwiches) then just follow their lead.

7. At attention. Don't slouch over your meal with your elbows on the table. Sitting up straight will make you look that much more interested in what's going on around you (even if you couldn't care less) — and it's *so* rude to act like you don't care.

8. **Chew on this.** Chewing with your mouth open is extremely unattractive — 'nuff said.

9. **Compliments work wonders.** Even if you don't like something being served, try a couple of bites. If anyone asks how you like it, you can honestly tell them you've never tasted anything quite like it. Then push the food around your plate to make it look like you've eaten more than you have.

10. **Take away.** Don't leave the table without thanking your hosts and offering to help clear up. Chances are they won't accept your offer to help since you're a guest but the offer will be appreciated.

Boys: Connect with Your Crush

The idea of talking to a boy, maybe even your crush, can sometimes seem more painful than a trip to the principal's office. What if he laughs at you, or worse, just walks away? But chances are he won't — because boys get just as nervous, honest. So instead of wasting time pretending not to notice him, strike up a convo. You might have a lot in common or nothing at all, but at least you've made a move.

1. When all else fails, smile. If you get totally tongue-tied every time he's near, don't worry about being the most brilliant conversationalist — just try smiling at him instead. A simple smile can speak volumes. But try to avoid a goofy ear-to-ear grin, 'cause he might worry that you've heard something funny about him and that the joke's on him!

2. Stand tall. Body language plays a big role in how others relate to you. Slouching, staring at the ground, or refusing to make eye contact shuts people out, even if it's not intentional. Boys are just as nervous as you are and might interpret your shy-girl stance as a lack of interest.

3. Common ground. If you're hoping to get to know someone, having some things in common sure does help. Find out what this boy's interests are. Of course, that doesn't mean faking a football fascination if watching games puts you to sleep (that's so lame). But knowing what position he plays, if you share an interest in books, or what he likes to do on weekends will make conversations easier.

4 **Stay focused.** Don't fall into the ditsy-girl trap. Melting into a puddle of drool while you're talking just isn't cool. Listen to what he has to say and come back with something smart. He'll respect you for it.

5 **School ties.** Attending the same school (or better yet, being in the same home-room) gives you an excuse to talk to him without the pressure of trying to find something fascinating to say. Just think of how many times during the day you have questions about homework or a sarcastic comment to make about the cafeteria mystery meat. So if he conveniently happens to be nearby, direct those comments his way to get a convo going.

6 **Play it cool.** While bumping into the boy you like every so often is cool, stalking him is so *not*. You want your encounters to be casual. He shouldn't feel like you've been following him around all day — that's just plain scary! And, yes, it *will* frighten him away.

7. Flattery will get you everywhere. Everyone likes to be praised for something they do well. Just look for stuff you admire about this boy, like the history report he read aloud in class or how well he played in last week's basketball game, and let him know you're impressed. But if you don't mean it and can't keep it sincere, then don't bother 'cause fake flattery is tacky (and usually pretty obvious).

8. Think positive. You're still going to be the same cool you, whether or not you and your crush hit it off. So don't pin your hopes and dreams onto one conversation with a boy who might not end up being all that after all. That way you won't be devastated if things don't work out.

9. Put yourself in his shoes. If you've caught him in an embarrassing moment — like he wiped out in the hall and ripped his pants — laugh it off and share your own horror story with him. Imagine how grateful you'd be if someone were this nice and sympathetic to you in your moment of disgrace.

10. **Have fun.** He's walking your way and you want to say something but your palms are sweating and your heart is racing. Wait a minute . . . it's not like you're about to perform brain surgery — you're just gonna make a little small talk. Remember, this is supposed to be fun. Take a deep breath, calm down, and enjoy yourself!

Does He Like You?

Boys can be pretty confusing. They can be chatty one minute and can clam up the next. Before you spend any more time drawing hearts around his name, make sure he's worthy of your admiration. A cute face isn't the only thing that counts.

1. **He calls.** Getting a phone call from a boy is major for three reasons: a) he knows your phone number or went to the trouble of looking it up; b) he dialed your number knowing your mom or bratty sister could always answer; and c) he called even though he knows you'll probably tell all your friends who will then tell all his friends. Give this boy a round of applause.

2. **He's thoughtful.** It might seem like he doesn't notice anything ("Hello, I streaked my hair blue!"), but if he comes through on the important stuff like sending you a birthday card or making you a mix of his favorite music, he's trying to show he likes you.

3. **He babbles.** If the boy of your dreams gets tongue-tied every time you're near, he's crushing. Keep in mind that boys get nervous, too. Unfortunately, if you notice that he sweats and stutters around *every* girl, then he might just be shy. Proceed with caution.

4. **His friends ask lots of questions.** Boys are just as shy as you are. He probably figures it's safer to have his friends find out about you first to make sure you even know he's alive. This way he doesn't risk going up to you and having you laugh in his face — that would be totally embarrassing. Not the most impressive technique, but at least he's trying.

5. **He gets close to your friend.** This smart guy knows the best way to get the 411 on you is to talk to your B.F. How do you know he's not just flirting with her? Easy. All he does is pump her for information about you.

6. **He stares at you.** Do you catch him staring in your direction, then quickly turning his head away when you spot him? Unless Michael Jordan or Mark McGwire is sitting behind you, it's a pretty safe bet that he's looking at you.

7. **He's always around.** He always seems to be right behind you in the lunch line or whenever you're walking into the library, he's walking out. And he must be clumsy because he's always bumping into you in the hallways. It's no coincidence — this boy wants you to notice him.

8. **He compliments you.** Just made a really good speech or played a good solo at the school concert? He's the first guy there telling you what a great job you did. Sweet.

9. **He asks about your plans.** When there's a party, a school dance, or even a fundraising car wash, your crush wants to know if you're going to be there. And he plays vague about his plans till he finds out about yours.

10. **He's nice.** If he's always making fun of you, don't take it as a sign of true love. Sure, everyone kids around but if you're feeling more harassed than flattered, tell this boy to buzz off. The boy who really likes you wants to make you laugh, not laugh at you.

Ten Excuses to Talk to a Boy

Can't find a thing to say to members of the male gender? Next time you're standing there and the cat's got your tongue, try these convo starters on for size.

1. **Ask him if he's played the newest Sony PlayStation game (which you've already mastered).** If he's into it, hopefully he'll start talking and a conversation will be happening.

2. **Tell him he reminds you of . . . (insert favorite athlete's name here).** He's probably more comfortable talking about sports and he'll appreciate the ego boost, too.

3. **Mention you're getting a soda and offer to get him one, too.** At least you will have made a conversational attempt and going to get the soda gives you a five-minute reprieve from having to make more small talk. It'll give you the chance to think of what you're gonna say when you get back.

4. **Ask to borrow his class notes (since you spent the whole class period staring at him).** He'll think you think he's smart.

5. **If he has missed class, when he gets back ask him if he'd like to borrow your notes (since you're a math whiz).**

6. **Stand behind him in the lunch line and ask him what animal he thinks the mystery meat comes from.**

7. **Ask him if he watched *the* game this weekend — any game will do.** But only ask if you're familiar with the game your-self so you can carry your end of the convo.

8. **Explain your conspiracy theory if he's an *X-Files* fan.**

9. **When he's talking to a mutual friend, join in on their conversation — the hard work of starting up a convo will already have been done.**

10. **Offer to tell his future by reading his palm.** Then find out how — fast.

How to Get Along with (Almost) Everybody

There will always be a couple of people in this world who you just don't get. That's OK, you don't have to be friends with everyone. But you may have to deal with these people you don't click with on a daily basis — she sits next to you at school or she's best friends with one of your friends — so you need to know how to get along with them anyway.

Here are some types of people you might encounter in life and ways to cope with them.

1. **The flake.** Every time you're supposed to get together she finds a reason for flaking out: Her mother won't let her go out, her cat is really sick, she needs to finish her homework, whatever. Without being mean about it, let her make the plans next time.

2. **The gossip.** She's got the scoop on everyone at school, from their latest crushes to who's in a big fight. No matter how nice she is, you know your secrets are never safe with her. Take a stand the next time she starts to blab about someone else's business — tell her you don't want to hear it.

3. **The do-gooder.** She's always got a smile on her face, even when she's down. She supports a bunch of causes and organizes all the events at school. Problem is, she's hard to get close to because she's so busy and underneath that brave face you never really know what she's thinking. Let her know she needs to spend less time looking out for others and more time taking care of herself.

4 **The teacher's pet.** She's the girl who asks for a pop quiz when the teacher doesn't have one planned or skips the school pep rally so she can study for a test (and makes sure everyone — especially teach — knows it). Studying hard is great, but this girl's trying way too hard to butter up the teacher. Don't let her get to you.

5 **The whiner.** This girl's always moaning and groaning about something, whether it's the weather, the school lunch, or homework. She's great if you need to vent about a horrible teacher but her constant complaining can really bring you down. The next time she gets going, try to change her attitude by pointing out the positive side of the situation.

6 **The shy girl.** You don't know much about her (no one does), but she sits next to you in class. And every time the teacher calls on her she turns bright red. Don't dismiss this girl because she doesn't speak up in class — she's just shy and is probably dying to make a friend. Make an extra effort to include her in your conversations. Once she gets comfortable around you, you might discover she'd make a great new friend.

7. The troublemaker. This girl's like a bad-luck charm. Rumors, lies, and accusations run wild when she's around. No one can put their finger on it but you think this scheming girl is at the center of it all. Run, don't walk, in the opposite direction the next time you see her coming or you could be her next victim.

8. The princess. Pretty and pampered, this girl is probably the least of your problems unless she asks you for something and you say no to her. She's so spoiled and used to getting her own way that she doesn't take kindly to those who don't do exactly what she wants. Should you bow down before her? No way. Without going out of your way to provoke her, the next time she makes an outrageous request, let her know where you stand.

9. The bully. This girl gets her way by intimidating anyone who stands up to her. She puts down others just for the fun of being in control. Don't play her game. She just wants to get you riled and when that doesn't happen she'll probably leave you alone. If the intimidation doesn't stop or gets worse, tell your parents or a teacher — don't fight this battle on your own.

10. The loner. She feels like an outcast, misunderstood. Maybe she dresses differently, listens to music no one else likes, or acts outrageously to shock. That doesn't mean she's not worth knowing. Try getting past the wall she's put up and let her know that while you might not share all her tastes you do have some basic stuff in common.

Chapter Two
On Your Own

Be Your Own Best Friend

Spending time with friends definitely rocks but that doesn't mean you should dread being alone. Even the most sociable people have to hang solo sometime. After all, how will you ever figure out what makes you happy if you're always compromising for the good of the group? So the next time you're spending an afternoon or evening alone, have a blast with your fave person — you!

1. Rainy day. If you're the type who's always saving baby-sitting money for a rainy day, well, now is the time to bust the piggy bank, baby. Treat yourself to something special 'cause you're worth it.

2. Happy Wednesday. Who needs an excuse to have fun? Celebrate random days, like Happy Wednesday or Good-luck Friday, by baking yourself chocolate chip cookies, painting your toenails with sparkles, renting a few of your fave flicks, or whatever rocks your world.

3. Hang ten. What better time to learn an extreme sport like surfing, snowboarding, or skateboarding? Girls are proving that these board sports are not just for boys and you'll feel superproud of yourself for learning to do something most people can't do.

4. Help out. Spend some time with people who would really benefit from it by volunteering at a nursing home or kids' day care center. Helping other people will make you feel oh so good about yourself, and hey, you won't be alone, either.

5. Slice of life. Look at life through a camera lens. If you don't have your own camera, ask your parents if you can borrow theirs, or get a disposable one. Walk around your neighborhood and snap shots of stuff that looks interesting. It'll help you get a whole new perspective on the world around you.

6. Get down. Always wanted to strum a guitar, play the piano, or bang on some bongos? Why not see if Mom will spring for some music lessons? If that's not in the budget, get a hold of a good manual and teach yourself. Knowing how to read and play music is a great skill to have.

7. Buff up. A buff is someone who's enthusiastic and knowledgeable about a specific subject. Become a buff on something really cool, like your favorite sport, author, or actor, for example. Search Web sites, read books or biographies, then dazzle your friends with your in-depth knowledge.

8. Far-off friends. Hanging solo doesn't mean you can't reach out to someone. Find yourself a pen pal, or even better, an e-pal who you can share letters with. Caution: But remember, when you find cyber friends, make sure you get to know them well before giving them any personal info. You might ask a grown-up you trust for advice here.

9. Quality time with the family. Your family doesn't need to know that all your friends are out of town. Let your parents think that you are playing with your little bro or sis because you truly want to, not because you have nothing better to do. They will be so impressed.

10. Movie night. The best part about renting a video on your own is that there's no arguing over who gets to pick the movie. So find your favorite flick, sit back, and enjoy.

Buh-bye to Shy

Ever feel like you're the only girl who blushes when speaking in class or talking to a boy? Well, you're not. Great, now what? Well, you may never be the loudest, boldest girl in class but here are some tips for squashing the butterflies in your stomach.

1. Write it out. Have to talk to your teacher about a make-up exam or maybe your parents are making you call your great-aunt to thank her for your birthday present? No need to panic — before you speak up, write yourself a few notes detailing exactly what you want to say. That way you won't totally forget what you were gonna say when you start speaking.

2. Be blame-free. Don't kick yourself every time you say something stupid. We all mess up. The harder you come down on yourself for not being the smoothest talker there is, the more difficult it'll be to speak up with confidence the next time. Go easy on yourself.

3. The power of thank-you. The next time someone compliments you on your hair or a new dress, pay attention to your response. Do you downplay every compliment with a negative comment like, "Really? I think I look terrible"? If someone says something nice, you owe it to them, and to yourself, to say thank-you. Accepting a compliment will help your self-esteem and boost your confidence.

4. You rule. Filled with doubt and bad feelings? Write down a list of everything you do well, even if it's something silly like washing the dishes. Consult this list every time you begin to think that maybe you can't do anything right — it'll help you remember just how many things you do *exactly* right.

5. Speak up. If you're filled with dread every time the teacher calls on you in class, don't sweat it. Just raise your hand when the subject is something you enjoy and are good at. It's easier to answer a question when you know you can't go wrong. Bonus: If you've already spoken up in class, the teacher will be less likely to pick on you later.

6. Draw the line. No matter how much you like your friends, if they make you feel bad about who you are, move on. You need friends who lift you up and boost your self-confidence.

7. New you. If the little stuff in life freaks you out, fuhgeddaboutit. Try conquering something that's intimidating to you. You don't have to bungee jump off a bridge, but do try out for the school play or train for your school's annual 10K roadrace. By conquering your fears, they'll have less control over you and you'll be more confident.

8. **Be prepared.** Instead of worrying about sounding stupid when talking to someone, plan ahead. Think of some questions you can ask in case there's a lull in the conversation. If you're prepared, you'll be less likely to blurt out something that you'll later regret.

9. **Help out.** Since you're already well acquainted with that tongue-tied feeling, go out of your way to help someone who's in the same boat. Find another shy person and strike up a conversation. You'll feel proud for having opened up and they'll appreciate your effort.

10. **Silence is golden.** You don't need to be the center of attention to be liked. So you're the quiet type — who cares? Being a good listener is a very cool quality to have — friends will appreciate it.

Feeling Down?

Does it seem like things aren't quite right in your life, only you can't put your finger on what's bothering you? Maybe you feel run-down a lot or get grumpy for no reason or just feel stressed-out and down. Check out the following signs of stress to see if you need to indulge in some serious chilling out, then read on for suggestions on how to get back on track. If a lot of these signs apply to you, talk to your parents or an adult you trust for help figuring out what's bringing you down big-time.

1. You constantly have knots in your stomach.

2. You lose your patience easily and snap at friends and family for no obvious reason.

3. You have trouble working up the energy to do anything.

4. You have a hard time falling asleep.

5. You are sleeping more than normal and have a hard time getting up in the morning.

6. Your back and neck muscles are tight.

7. The stuff that used to make you smile isn't really fun anymore.

8. You feel sad a lot.

9. It's hard for you to make decisions or commit to a project.

10. You've lost — or gained — a lot of weight.

Turn That Frown Upside Down

When you're down, it can seem like things will never ever get better. The trick to beating the blues is to try to stay positive and prevent them from happening in the first place. That said, if you're already in the middle of a big old funk, you need to figure out how to pull yourself out. Simple stuff like exercising and eating right can help but if things just seem to keep getting worse, never doubt the power of talking to a friend or adult you trust.

1. Write it down. During happy moments make a list of all the things that make you feel good. That way you can consult the list when things seem bleak to (hopefully) raise your spirits.

2. Sweat it out. There are many benefits to exercise, one of which is the fact that working up a good sweat and getting your blood pumping will make you feel better. So boost your mood by slipping on some sneakers and hitting the pavement.

3. Talk about it. Find someone you can really trust, like a friend or favorite teacher, and open up. Knowing that you're not facing things all alone can be a big help.

4. Eat right. Don't go on a junk-food binge to soothe your bad feelings. The sugar rush won't last long and you'll only crash even harder. Make sure you get the vitamins and protein you need to stay healthy and have plenty of energy.

5. Breathe. Make like a *yogini* (a girl who practices yoga) and breathe. Sure, you already know how to breathe, but what about deep, relaxing breaths? Practice this breathing method — it'll help calm you down.

6. Worry constructively. Instead of spending all your time worrying about and rehashing what's past, work on what you can do in the present. Devote your energy to coming up with a solution to your problems.

7. Dear diary. Not ready to share your thoughts with anyone else just yet? Write down your worries in a journal. You'll feel good about getting stuff out of your system and then you can go back later and read what you wrote with a more objective outlook. This might help you sort through what's bothering you.

8. Good vs. bad. Faced with a big decision that's got you anxious, like whether or not you should let your friend know someone's been spreading gossip about her? Write down the pros and cons (reasons why it would be best to tell her and then also why it might be best if she didn't know) and then look over the list to help you figure out which decision is best overall.

9. **Help out.** Volunteering to help others can make you feel better about yourself. Nothing will take your mind off your problems faster than finding someone who's worse off than you. It can also help you realize that maybe your problems aren't so bad after all.

10. **Rock out.** Lock your bedroom door, take the phone off the hook, and put on some of your favorite music. It may be a temporary solution but for at least an hour you'll forget about your problems and get lost in the music.

Get Mad (and Get Over It)

Best friends never fight, right? Wrong. But it's healthy to share your feelings, even if they're negative, because getting stuff out in the open helps resolve problems. Of course, that doesn't mean insulting or abusing the other person — that's *always* wrong.

1. Think it over. Are you gearing up for WW III or just a minor conflict? Before you confront anyone, look at how this argument rates on the friendship foul-up scale. Forgetting to return your phone call isn't worthy of a showdown. Keep that in mind when you bring up what's bothering you.

2. Whose fault is it? Examine what really made you mad in the first place. That way you can focus on the issue instead of blaming your friend for every little thing that's gone wrong in your life, when most of it doesn't have anything to do with her.

3. Don't simmer in silence. You need to share your feelings with your friend or it'll create a void between you. After all, she may not even know that she's offended you (she's not a mind reader). Explain how you feel and then give her the chance to make it up to you.

4. Explain, don't blame. Whatever you do, don't explode and just start angrily accusing your friend of all kinds of stuff. Also try to avoid words like *always* and *never* — this will just put her on the defensive and won't get you any closer to repairing your friendship. Try to be reasonable and listen to her side of the story.

5. **Get it out.** If, at a particular moment, you don't think you can express yourself clearly, there are other, more private ways to vent your anger. Pound your pillow, run around the block a couple of times, yell and cry if you want to — just get it out of your system, because those bitter feelings can be poison and make the situation even more grim.

6. **Find another friendly ear.** Want to talk but can't trust yourself just yet to confront your friend without screaming at her? Find an objective listener (a parent, teacher, or another friend), and pour out your heart to them. They might be able to point out something you hadn't thought of before (maybe your friend isn't at fault after all) and help you figure out how best to patch things up.

7. Write it out. You can develop your own objective view on the situation by writing your feelings in a journal. After you've expressed yourself, put your journal away for a while, then go back and read it with fresh eyes — it might help you get a clearer take on the situation.

8. Don't seek revenge. Revenge isn't really sweet and will just make you suffer more. Humiliating or hurting a friend who hurt you just to get her back won't do anything but cause more negativity and bad feelings.

9. Forgive and try to forget. Even if you don't really want to, you should forgive your friend (especially once she apologizes or explains). Holding a grudge will only keep the incident fresh in your mind and cause more pain. If you don't think your friendship can survive the incident, you'll have to deal with it — but staying angry won't help.

10. Move on. You've confronted your friend, explained your feelings, she apologized, and the two of you made up — now get over it. Don't use her past mistakes against her to make her feel bad every time she does something you don't like. If you can't stop throwing the past in her face, ask yourself if you really want to be friends — this may be your way of trying to end the friendship without you even realizing it. (Of course, if you treat her poorly, she might end the friendship before you do.)

Get Your Point Across

When you're speaking to people, do you stare at the ground and slowly lose steam halfway through a sentence? Having a conversation seems like a no-brainer but it does take effort to communicate clearly and get your point across. Don't worry, nobody is waiting for you to say something brilliant — just say what you want to say clearly and well.

1. Don't get distracted. When you're talking on the phone, no matter how hungry you are or which great TV show is on, don't eat or try to watch the tube at the same time. No way will you be able to successfully carry on your half of the convo if you are so distracted. If you really can't control your cravings, tell your friend you'll call her back after you've eaten (or when the show's over).

2. Don't interrupt. You know how annoying it is to be in the middle of telling a story only to be interrupted by one of your friends. Well, if you show some respect and don't interrupt others, then hopefully they'll get the message and treat you the same way.

3. One at a time. Even if your problems seem much worse, pay attention while your friend is speaking and do your best to listen to what she's saying. That way when it's your turn to speak, you'll know where she stands and you'll be better able to keep her attention. There'll be plenty of time to talk about your feelings once she's done.

4. Short and sweet. No matter how much other people go on about themselves during a conversation, don't follow their lead and bore everyone with details they really don't need to know. If you've got a story to tell, you'll hold your friends' interest much more if you get it out quickly and clearly.

5. Plan ahead. Have a hard time thinking of stuff to say? The next time you hear something funny or freaky, make a mental note to tell someone about it later or even write it down so you'll remember to share it — it'll make your retelling much clearer and more effective.

6. Eye contact. Your body language can be interpreted in many different ways. People could think you're bored, snobby, shy, or even clueless if you avoid making eye contact and shuffle from one foot to the other while you're talking. So stand up straight and look them in the eye the next time you've got something to say and people will be much more likely to listen.

7. Different strokes. Keep people's personalities in mind when you're talking to them. If you're telling an embarrassing story to someone supersensitive, she may end up getting offended rather than seeing the humor in the situation.

8. Bad habits. Keep the "uhs" to a minimum — they just distract people from hearing what you're really trying to say.

9. Silent clues. Always pay attention to the body language and verbal cues other people are displaying. There may be something they're not telling you — like they're in a superrush and therefore not really paying one hundred percent attention to what you're saying — that could save you from going on and on. Hold it for another time when your audience is all ears.

10. Don't be a critic. Even if you think your friends are wrong, don't contradict what they're saying or correct their grammar. That's a job for their parents or English teacher, not you. They'll be more likely to tune you out if they think everything you've got to say is critical.

Chapter Three
On the Home Front

Raising Cool Parents (or How to Get What You Want)

While you may not always agree with your parents, you do have to find a way to coexist peacefully. Use your smarts — your parents are most likely rational people so if you reason with them on their level, they'll be more likely to change the rules in your favor.

1. Ready, set, negotiate. Try to negotiate with your parents to change the rules before you go and break one of them. After all, they just may understand your point of view and be willing to change or bend the rules. If you do get caught breaking a rule, tough luck. You knew you weren't supposed to do it in the first place.

2. Be generous. Give as much as you take. If Mom lets you stay out extra late one night, let her know you appreciate the gesture, then stay home the next night and do the dishes.

3. Clue them in. Parents always want to know what's going on with you, so keep Mom and Dad as informed as possible. If you're not sure where you're going to be, at least give them the names and numbers of the people you'll be meeting. They'll be less likely to worry — and if they're not worried, they won't be as mad when you're five minutes late coming home.

4. Work it out. Don't waste time complaining about everything you can't do. Brooding never got anyone anywhere. Instead spend your time either doing the fun stuff you *are* allowed to do or else figuring out how to come to a new understanding with your parents.

5. Say you're sorry. If you've messed up, admit you're wrong and accept the punishment your parents feel fits the crime. You can always try to negotiate the terms of your grounding later on — right now you need to appear as sorry as possible.

6. Chill out. You know you're not a little girl anymore even if your parents still see you as their baby. Don't explode if they seem stuck in the past — it'll be way more productive if you calmly explain how you feel and then give them a chance to catch up.

7. Body talk. You think you're paying attention, but your parents think you're disrespecting them. What's going on here? It could all be in your body language. Rolling your eyes and shrugging your shoulders sends negative nonverbal cues to your folks. Act more grown-up by making eye contact and standing tall the next time you're talking with your parents and they'll be less likely to treat you like a little kid.

8. Playback. Parents, being who they are, believe they're giving you the best advice possible. So the next time you're discussing some heavy issues, listen carefully to what they have to say. Then let them know you understand how they feel by repeating their concerns before bringing up your own points. At least then they'll know you're listening and will be much more likely to hear you out in return.

9. Don't compare. Don't tell your parents you should be allowed to do something because all your friends do — it's the kiss of death. Who knows why, but it just doesn't work.

10. Be choosy. Fight the battles worth fighting. Convincing your parents to let you go to the last school dance of the year is something worth pushing for, but being allowed to see a movie on a weeknight probably just isn't worth the hassle of a battle. Save your efforts for when it's really important.

(Surviving Your Siblings)

Grown-ups always claim you'll appreciate your brothers and sisters when you get older — as if the day after your twenty-first birthday all feuds will be forgotten and you'll be the best of friends. Whatever! Right now you're just trying to get them out of your stuff and out of your room without starting WW III.

1.) Don't freak out. Avoid major battle scenes, for example, screaming or throwing things, 'cause you'll end up getting the blame even if it wasn't your fault.

2.) Kill 'em with kindness. Are your sibs absolutely driving you up a wall? Smile sweetly and keep your mouth shut. They'll stop pestering you if it seems like they're not having an effect on you.

3.) An eye for an eye. Sis flushed your brush down the toilet? Don't look for revenge by tossing her favorite headband in the trash — it'll only keep the fight going. And besides, if you just walk away in the face of her childish act, you'll look that much more mature (especially to your parents) — and that could definitely help out in the long run.

4.) Rules to live by. Whether you just live in the same house or — horrors — have to share a bedroom, establish some ground rules you both agree to live by, like no borrowing each other's stuff without permission, etc.

5. **Battle zone.** Don't, under any circumstances, hit your brother or sister. No one deserves to be abused no matter how mad their behavior makes you. And your parents will absolutely *not* approve.

6. **The blame game.** If you ruined your sister's skirt or broke your brother's fish tank you should apologize and accept responsibility for what you've done. Denying any involvement is pretty pathetic when you're the obvious culprit. Avoiding responsibility will just end up making things worse.

7. **In their eyes.** If you've got little brothers and sisters, do your best to be a great role model. Show them how you'd like to be treated by treating them with respect and you'll establish a good relationship that can be carried into the future.

8. **Who knew?** Every once in a while spend some time actually talking to your siblings — you might be surprised to find out you don't know them as well as you thought and that, hey, you like them!

9. **The friends factor.** Never humiliate your sibs in front of their friends no matter how mad you are at them 'cause they'll just return the favor when your friends are over. Keep family problems in the family — your sibling rivalry is no one else's business.

10. **Tune out.** You've pleaded to be left alone, you've threatened to go to your folks, but still your brother or sister won't stop bothering you. Before you throw a major fit, walk away and lock yourself in your bedroom or, if you share a room, maybe even the bathroom for some private time.

Redo Your Room

It doesn't have to cost a ton of dough to give your room the boost it needs to go from boring to beautiful. You spend a lot of time there, so you might as well have it exactly how you want it!

1. Keep it clean. Keeping your bedroom clean isn't just a parental plot against you — you'll be happy you've tidied up because you'll have more space, your room will look better, and it'll get rid of allergy-inducing dust bunnies.

2. Use it or lose it. Before you buy anything new that's gonna end up living in your room, look around to see if there's anything you can get rid of. Overflowing dressers and chaotic closets are not attractive and won't help you be organized, either. Follow the six-month rule — if you haven't worn or used something in the past six months, it's gotta go. If you're really having a hard time permanently parting with your stuff, hide it in storage under your bed. If you don't miss it after two months (out of sight, out of mind) then you really should get rid of it to make way for any new stuff.

3. Stash it. Just can't bring yourself to part with stuffed animals, old birthday cards, and souvenirs of the family vacay you took three years ago? Pack mementos into crates or baskets and stash them where they can't be seen and won't get in the way. Keep a night-stand by the bed so you can store magazines, books, and other essentials you want close at hand.

4. **Good karma.** Try practicing a little *feng shui* (pronounced *fung shway*). This an-cient Chinese art of organization infuses your room with good karma. The logic is if you're comfortable with the space you spend the most time in — your room — then you'll find harmony and balance in the rest of your life. Visit your local library to find books on *feng shui* and learn how to get your bedroom's cos-mic forces aligned.

5. **Recycle your stuff.** Got a lamp shade you don't like anymore or an ugly old chair taking up room as a makeshift clothes hanger (but you never actually sit on the thing)? Get creative. Glue plastic flowers to your lamp shade or cover it with a collage of your fa-vorite images to make it more you. Paint a whole new pattern on the chair or cover it with a cool throw. A little imagination could be the key to a brand-new bedroom.

6. Little things. Say you've got some cash to buy some new stuff for your room but it's not quite enough for big-ticket items like new furniture. Don't fret — you don't have to break the bank to make a major difference. A couple of inexpensive lamps, a new set of sheets, or a funky blanket or pillows thrown across the bed go a long way.

7. Color me happy. Colors set the mood of a room so choose carefully — the pink you love today could make you sick tomorrow. Orange, red, pink, and yellow make a room feel warm and cozy, while blues and greens will make your room seem bigger and brighter. If Mom and Dad refuse to let you paint the walls your favorite shade of bright purple, find accessories in this color that you can scatter around the room. A little color goes a long way.

8. Find a theme. Narrow your interests down to a theme, like Hawaiian surfer girl or big-city bookworm. Then you can start hunting for bits and pieces to make your room more interesting: ornaments, posters, memorabilia, etc. Friends will be fascinated by your well-thought-out decorating scheme.

9. **Plaster it.** Give your room an original, personal look by hanging some cool art posters on your wall among your favorite pics of movie and music stars. Or paint your own pictures or get an artistic friend to create something for your walls.

10. **Shake it up.** Can't afford anything new and the 'rents have threatened to disown you if you paint the place? No worries. With a couple of hours and some hard labor you can get your room looking like new by totally re-arranging the furniture. Even if it's just switching everything from one side of the room to the other, at least you'll have a new perspective when you go to bed at night.

Family Fun

Stop the presses — it *is* possible to have fun with your family without any presents or major holidays involved. Playing video games together, going to the park and tossing a Frisbee around, or taking a road trip might end up being fun after all (surprise!) and could even put you in a laid-back holiday state of mind.

1. Special screening. Gonna watch a movie you rented? You might opt to invite the folks to watch it with you.

2. Get cooking. Try making something fun together for dinner. If you don't usually help with the cooking, offer to lend a hand; if you do normally help cook, suggest a recipe your family's never tried before or a really rich dessert for a special treat.

3. Playtime. Invite the folks to a rousing game of Monopoly or another board game. Or if you have a Sony PlayStation, introduce them to modern technology by teaching them how to play your fave game.

4. Get crazy. How wild will Mom and Dad get? Could you talk them into a whomping pillow fight or an all-out water fight? Go for it.

5. Outdoor adventure. Get outdoors and go for a bike ride, take a trip to the local pool, play a game of volleyball or tag football, or just go fly a kite — but do it together.

6. Get organized. Join forces to tackle a household project — like sorting all those loose photos and putting them into an album or cleaning out the garage. It may not be the most thrilling activity but it'll get done faster if you all lend a hand. And you never know — it may end up being fun after all!

7. Talk to one another. Share a joke you heard at school, tell them what's on your mind, or ask them how their day went — just get the conversation going.

8. Home movies. Record a videotape of your family that you can send to Grandma or another relative and the whole family will feel closer.

9. Getaway. Plan a vacation, picnic, or road trip together. It doesn't have to be expensive, just a cool outing everyone can share.

10. Mix it up. Swap tapes with your parents and give their favorite music a listen while they listen to your fave tunes. You may begin to understand one another's musical tastes. Try not to laugh so hard you fall to the floor when you hear *their* music.

(A Pet's Best Friend)

Animals don't expect much — some food, a little scratching behind the ears, and a warm bed — yet they give so much in return. Don't take your pet for granted — treat it well and do everything you can to make it happy.

1. **Find the time.** If you're considering getting a pet, make sure you can look after it properly. All pets, even cats who seem totally independent, need loving care. If the animal is supposed to be your responsibility, don't slack off or forget and then just assume Mom will save the day by doing the walking, feeding, or cage cleaning herself. That's not cool.

2. **Two's company.** Hamsters like living solo, while rabbits prefer lots of company. Do your research and make sure you give your pet the living situation that'll make it happiest.

3. **It's a jungle out there.** You might have visions of all your animals living together happily ever after but make sure you don't introduce a new animal into the bunch that might hurt or even kill another one of your pets (like cats with hamsters or big fish with much littler fish, for example).

4. **Have a heart.** Adopt your animal from a shelter and give an abandoned animal a loving home. Be sure to have your dog or cat neutered or spayed so you help control the pet population.

5. **Don't poison your pets.** Don't feed your pets human food even if they beg for it because there's lots of seemingly harmless stuff that they just can't digest and it can cause serious problems. Spices, dairy food, and even chocolate can poison your precious pet.

6. **Kibbles 'n Bits.** Can't figure out what your pet should eat? Consult your vet about the amount and type of food Fido should be eating. Most animals love to eat, so if they aren't getting excited at mealtimes, there may be something wrong.

7. Home sweet home. Unless your pet lives in a stable and answers to the name Black Beauty, try to avoid locking them out of the house or shutting them in a room by themselves for long periods of time. Most animals are social creatures by nature and will get lonely if forced to live alone outside.

8. We are family. Most dogs like to be treated as a member of the family. They see you as their parent and primary caregiver. So get down on the floor, roll around, and play with them to make them feel loved.

9. Call of the wild. Don't rely solely on your backyard or your apartment complex's minipark for your dog's sole exercise and entertainment. Confining Spot to one place will bore him. Dogs need to roam, explore new neighborhoods, and play with other dogs in order to get the exercise they need and to learn how to behave properly as well.

{10.} Scrub some suds. Even if your cat or dog fights like crazy at the sight of a bathtub, groom them on a regular basis. Domestic pets can carry parasites like ticks and fleas that can infest your house and make you sick. Having their ears checked and keeping their teeth clean will also help them live longer, happier, and healthier lives. And if your pet is a cage-dweller, make sure to clean its home thoroughly once a month.

Chapter Four
Healthy Habits

Daily Fitness

Getting fit isn't about building the perfect biceps or losing weight — it's about being active and healthy, and it's a choice you make daily: stairs or the elevator, fries or fruit, walking to the corner store or begging for a ride. Making the right choices now will pay off big-time in the future.

1. Set goals. Why do you want to get in shape? Are you training for the track team? Do you have a hiking trip planned with friends and want to be able to get through it without huffing and puffing the whole way? Working toward a goal will give you extra motivation and you'll accomplish more with a schedule than without one.

2. **Reward yourself.** Every time you reach a goal, give yourself credit and let others know how well you're doing. Don't be bashful — getting in shape is a reason to celebrate!

3. **Stair-mistress.** Take the stairs over an escalator or elevator whenever possible. It firms up your calves, quads, and butt and gets that heart pumping, too.

4. **Door-to-door.** Instead of having Mom drive you door-to-door, ask her to drop you off a couple of blocks from school or the mall and walk the rest of the way at a fast pace — it'll work your heart and lungs and rev up your metabolism.

5. **Stretch it out.** Next time you find yourself on a mega phone marathon or spending the evening in front of the TV, use some of that time to stretch out muscles — being flexible and limber helps you perform better in sports and makes you feel better, too.

6. Clean up. Okay, so it may sound like a parental plot, but it's not — cleaning your room tones your muscles and improves your flexibility, too.

7. Fitness for fun. Drag along a friend and join a dance class. It'll make your workouts more fun and will inspire both of you to keep going.

8. "I love this game." Find something physical that you enjoy doing. It's much more likely that you'll stick with an activity if you're having fun doing it. And you're not going to get fit by quitting and sitting around doing nothing.

9. Practice makes perfect. Don't give up if the results of your new-found athleticism aren't instant. Once you've started your exercise routine, it'll take at least three months to see any noticeable changes.

10. Bonus. There *are*, however, some benefits to exercise you'll enjoy almost as soon as you start working out, like getting a good night's sleep, feeling stronger and healthier, and having more energy.

Get Some Sleep

Some people have no problem catching their z's but many others toss and turn their way through the night. Lack of sleep can make you look and feel rotten, never mind that your catnaps during class are going to get you in big trouble. Try changing some of your before-bed habits and you'll soon find yourself in dreamland.

1. Sweet dreams. Have a cup of warm milk with honey before bed. They both contain tryptophan, a natural chemical that gets you nice and drowsy and can help you sleep.

2. Rock till you drop. Wear yourself out with a game of tag football or tennis after dinner — or groove around your room to the beat of your favorite song. But avoid exercise right before bed or else you'll be too pumped up to sleep.

3. Easy does it. Stay away from the spicy stuff at dinner. Your rumbling stomach will keep you awake all night long. Try not to stuff yourself, either — being too full can keep you up, too.

4. Same time, same place. Try to hit the sack at the same time every day. The more your body is used to a routine, the faster you'll be off to dreamland.

5. Keep it quiet. Don't watch TV in bed. If your body associates bedtime with action movies or weepy dramas, you'll never fall asleep. The quieter and calmer your bedtime routine, the better.

6. Baa-baa-boring. If you can't sleep, don't lie there forever counting sheep. After 15 minutes, get up and change your scenery for a few minutes or read quietly in bed, then try again.

7. Catnap. Nothing's wrong with a quick afternoon nap but (unless you're getting sick) sleeping any longer than half an hour could seriously throw off your body clock and almost guarantee a sleepless night.

8. Do not disturb. Turn the ringer on your phone off so you won't be disturbed by incoming calls. Let any family members who are still up know that you are trying to get some shut-eye so they'll know not to bother you or make too much noise.

9. Catch up. Make up for a few late nights by going to bed extra-early the next few.

10. Get real. Don't doze off in front of the TV or force yourself to keep your eyes open just because there's a great movie on or your friends want to come over. Go to bed when you're tired — your body will thank you for it.

(Eat Smart)

The key to a good diet is eating *smart*, not less. Diets generally don't work because they make you hungry (duh) and cause your metabolism (which is in charge of burning calories) to slow down so you end up having to eat less and less so as not to gain weight. And that usually backfires. It makes more sense to fill up on good-for-you grub — and don't fool yourself into thinking that eating an entire fat-free cheesecake isn't bad for you. 'Cause it is.

_1._ Food is fuel. Don't eat if you're not hungry. Food can't take the place of love or friendship. Its purpose is to give fuel to the body so don't make the mistake of letting food mean more than it is.

_2._ Pace yourself. Not sure if you should finish what's on your plate? Take a break before you feel totally full since it takes a while for your stomach to feel full to you (even when it really is). If you're still hungry after waiting a while, then it's probably fine to eat some more. Pay attention to what your stomach is telling you.

_3._ Breakfast rules. Don't speed off for the school bus without breakfast. Studies show it helps you do a lot better in school if you have some fuel in your body before the day starts.

_4._ Fat-free fakes. Don't chow down on low-fat or fat-free foods thinking they don't count because they're certainly not calorie-free. These semi-tasteless treats also aren't as satisfying so you end up wanting to eat more of the mediocre stuff. And they also tend to

have lots of false stuff in 'em (like preserva-
tives) that aren't healthy.

5. **Avoid jumbo portions.** Don't supersize those fries. Compared to portions in
some other countries like England, American
portions are almost double the size. An aver-
age steak or serving of nachos here in the U.S.
would be considered jumbo-sized overseas.
So if you're always getting the extra-large por-
tion you're eating way more at one time than
most people consider normal.

6. **No more meat.** Going veggie is a
valid, healthy lifestyle choice but make sure
you find out how to supplement the protein
and other nutrients you might be missing
when you banish meat from your diet.

7. **Everything in moderation.** Don't
overdose on the sweet stuff, but you might
not want to cut it out of your diet completely. Even if you want to eliminate sugar
one hundred percent, avoiding any type of
food completely is very difficult to maintain

and could backfire — you might end up with cravings that result in a major pig-out.

8. Checklist. Check the ingredients of what you're buying. Generally the first ingredient listed on the label is the highest in quantity. For example, if you're buying juice and the first ingredient is sugar, put it back on the shelf because there's hardly any actual juice in it. Try to buy foods where the first ingredient is something healthy, or at least not a nasty preservative.

9. Go for the greens. Look for fruits and vegetables that are darker in color — like spinach instead of iceberg lettuce or yams over regular potatoes — because they're usually the better sources of vitamins and minerals.

10. Food for thought. Eat with a conscience: Make sure you buy tuna that's dolphin-safe (meaning no dolphins were caught and hurt in tuna nets), look for free-range chickens and eggs (that means chickens that aren't caged and are naturally grain fed), and support your local farmers by buying their produce.

Exercise Excuses

"I'd love to get in shape but it's too cold outside to do anything." "I'd like to be stronger but I can never get to the free weights because there are so many guys around at the gym." "Why exercise? I tried once and nothing happened."

Any of these excuses sound familiar? Read on to see why these bogus lines don't hold up.

1. "It hurts." Forget the "no pain, no gain" slogan. If you're really that sore then maybe it's time to change your routine. If you're doing something intense, like kick-boxing, switch to something less high-impact, like swimming or speed-walking — these activities are less likely to cause aches and pains.

2. "I'm too tired." You might feel awful the first morning you get up to exercise or feel pooped at the end of the day but things will get easier. Once you experience the energy boost you get from exercise, you'll want to continue working out. So get off the couch and get moving!

❸ "I'm embarrassed." Can't figure out how to use the equipment at the gym so you feel like a dork and want to give up completely? Relax. Ask one of the pros, that's what they're there for. Feel like you should be in better shape before taking an aerobics class or else you'll make a fool of yourself? Forget it — a lot of other people are probably beginners, too.

❹ "It's too cold or hot outside." Thank goodness for the VCR. If the weather is stopping you from exercising outdoors, pop in a workout tape and turn your living room into an aerobics studio.

❺ "It takes too long to get results." It will take at least three months to see serious results in the muscle-building category, but you'll start feeling better immediately. Focus on the short-term benefits, like the extra energy you have or the good feeling you get after a really sweaty session.

6. **"It's boring."** If you're not having fun, stop doing what you're doing and find an activity you like to do. Don't force yourself to run lap after lap around the track if it feels like torture — maybe hiking, mountain biking, or even modern dance class is more your style. The more you enjoy a routine or activity, the more likely you are to stick with it.

7. **"I'll start next month . . . next Monday . . . after my birthday . . ."** Don't set a specific date for beginning to work out because that'll put way too much pressure on you to perform. Besides, there's no time like the present! Start right now (or at least tomorrow morning if you're already in bed) — do a couple of sit-ups, walk around the block, or shoot some hoops at least. Hey, something is better than nothing.

8. **"I would work out but I already messed up and ate a chocolate bar."** Don't blow the rest of the day just because you pigged out in the morning. Every minute of the day is a chance to start all over again. Anyway, what better reason to exercise than to work off those greasy fries you had at lunch?

9. **"I can't afford to join a gym."** You don't need lots of fancy equipment to get in shape. Cans of corn can be turned into free weights and it doesn't cost anything to run or walk, right?

10. **"I'm too busy."** You'll always be busy, it's just a matter of setting priorities. How important to you is your health?

Chapter Five
Beauty Basics

Banish Bad Hair Days

Bad hair days can seem like the end of the world. But before you throw in the towel, have faith and read on — things *can* get better. A little conditioner here, a trim there, and even you can have happy, shiny, healthy hair.

1. Come in from the cold. Cold weather can make hair dry and unmanageable — static cling, anyone? So give it a double dose of moisture by using a moisturizing shampoo and conditioner on a regular basis, then giving your hair a weekly deep conditioner or hot oil treatment.

2. Untangle yourself. By combing your hair before you shampoo, you'll have fewer tangles when you're done. To be truly tangle-free, gently comb again after you've applied conditioner, then rinse.

3. Lather, rinse, and rinse again. Is your hair always dull, even after you've just washed it? Make sure you're rinsing all the shampoo suds out of your hair. Shampoo residue can kill even the best head of hair — so spend at least two minutes rinsing.

4. Curls are us. If you're putting hair products, like mousse or gel, into curly hair, don't rub or pull the product through your hair 'cause that'll cause frizzies. Instead, gently scrunch the product into the ends of your hair for beautiful curls.

5. Bag it. If you're suffering from serious split ends, your purse or backpack could be to blame. Next time you sling your bag over your shoulder, make sure it's not catching your hair — it could be causing major breakage and damage.

6. When snipping is the only solution. If you already have split ends, the only way to get rid of them is to trim them off. But you can try to prevent them in the future by spraying your hair with a leave-in conditioner and keeping your hair dryer on low heat and eight to ten inches from your head when you blow-dry.

7. Wet-head. Two common mistakes people make when blow-drying are starting too early, so soaking wet hair gets blown to death, or else leaving the job half done (hello, frizzies!). Start by towel-drying your hair to get rid of any excess moisture, then blow-dry till hair is one hundred percent dry, not damp!

8. Give yourself some space. To avoid burnout, hold the dryer at least eight to ten inches from your hair when you're drying it. You can move in a little closer, say four to six inches from your hair, if you're styling it.

9. Point and shoot. Aim the air flow from your dryer down the length of your hair.

It'll prevent hair cuticles from getting ruffled up, so hair will end up smoother and shinier.

10. **Strong hair is happy hair.** If you like to wear your hair in a ponytail, try to avoid tying it the same way every day. Your hair will get weaker and be more likely to break if it's secured in the same spot every time. It's also a good idea to use a no-snag hair elastic for pulling hair back — these are easy to remove and won't break off a chunk of hair in the process.

(Fashion Don'ts)

You can make a million fashion mistakes that aren't going to help you look your best — like wearing white socks with strappy sandals. But looking good is just as much about attitude as it is about wardrobe — wear your clothes with confidence and people are unlikely to criticize.

1. **Beware fancy footwear.** Don't supersize your shoe selection when you're wearing something simple like shorts or capris (also called clam-diggers and pedal pushers). Match them up with sneakers or flats and stay away from strappy heels, which will just look silly.

2. Push and pull. Don't buy jeans you barely fit into, hoping to lose weight. Shrinkage is unavoidable with new jeans so don't buy 'em too tight. To minimize the amount they should shrink, however, you can try washing them inside out with the button fastened and the zipper closed and always tumble dry on low heat. You can also take them out of the dryer before they're fully dry and hang them up to air dry.

3. Keep it clean. If your clothes smell or have really noticeable stains, wash them already. Being dirty is just gross.

4. Smelly feet. Don't wear the same shoes every day. It's not really a fashion faux pas, but bacteria builds up more quickly if your shoes don't get a chance to breathe, leading to major stinkage. Pee-uww.

5. Once is not enough. Don't buy anything that you can't ever see yourself wearing

more than once, unless it's a formal dress —
and even then try to get something that you
could wear at another occasion, too.

6. **Comfort is key.** Too short, too tight,
missing buttons, an unidentifiable stain, falling hems — we've all been victims of dressing
disasters. Don't leave home unless you feel
completely comfortable with what you're
wearing because tugging on the back of your
skirt or trying to hide a hole under the arm of
a shirt is going to make you feel miserable all
day long.

7. **Shop smart.** Don't go shopping without giving your existing wardrobe a once-over
first. You might already own the perfect top
that just needs a boost and pairing it with a
new pair of jeans might do the trick (and save
you the cost of a new shirt).

8. **Cheap chic.** You don't have to update
your wardrobe every season, no matter what
the fashion experts say. Save money by buying
some new accessories — like handbags, rings,
bracelets, hair stuff, etc. — and dress up the
clothes you already have with some new extras.

9. **Discount duds.** Don't waste your money on useless sales when you don't really need the items in the first place, bargain or not. You'll just end up tossing that stuff to the back of your closet and will have to spend more money to get what you really wanted in the first place. Stay focused on what you really need when you shop.

10. **Bubble-licious.** Don't throw away a perfectly good shirt just because there's gum stuck to it. Seal the shirt in a plastic bag and put it in a freezer overnight. Ta-da — you'll be able to pick the gum off in the morning.

Good Grooming

Just because you're too young to wear makeup doesn't mean there aren't things you can do to look prettier. You don't need mascara and lipstick to look beautiful—clean, shiny hair, clear skin, fresh breath, and well-kept nails make a great impression. So let your natural beauty shine through!

1. **Wash up.** Your skin produces oil constantly so you should wash your face twice a day — when you wake up and before bed. But don't make the mistake of overscrubbing because that will just irritate your skin and could dry it out. Wash with a mild soap that won't dry out or irritate your skin.

2. **Rinse regularly.** Rinse your facecloth well every time you use it so you don't get a soap build-up, then throw it in the washing machine every couple of days to get it really clean. After all, this thing is touching your face on a daily basis — you don't want mildewy soap scum on it, do you?

3. **Moisturize.** Apply a light moisturizer right after washing your face or getting out of the shower. Your skin loses water every day (even faster during the winter) and moisturizer helps hold the water in longer and makes your skin feel softer.

4. **Speaking of water . . .** Since your body is made up mostly of water, be kind to it by replenishing its supply. Your body loses water constantly during the day (and night), especially if you're sweating or playing sports — so drink eight glasses of the stuff daily. Water helps keep your skin and hair looking good.

5. **Don't overdo it.** Even if you've got oily hair, don't wash it more than once a day. Turns out "lather, rinse, and repeat" really isn't all that good for you — it removes too many of your hair's natural oils.

6. **Fingers and toes.** Having a layer of dirt under your nails could make even the strongest stomach churn. Keep your fingernails and toenails clipped and clean.

7. **Sparkling smile.** Brush and floss at least twice a day to keep your teeth and gums healthy and your smile at its best. If you have braces, you should be brushing after every meal to make sure no food gets stuck in the wiring.

8. **Trim time.** Have your hair trimmed regularly to make tresses easier to tame and to get rid of scraggly split ends.

9. **Daily douse.** Take a bath or shower every day and make sure to actually wash with soap — don't just let the water run over you and call yourself clean — it's the soap that does the job.

10. **Don't touch.** Don't pick at scabs, pimples, or any other skin irritation because it could cause a permanent scar to form. Instead wash or treat the area gently and then leave it alone to heal.

Health and Beauty Whoppers

There are some wild, sometimes funny, but definitely misleading health and beauty tips out there that just don't work. Some are a bummer to uncover but others are definitely good news.

1. **Sit-ups will give you killer abs. False.** Sit-ups will strengthen your stomach muscles but won't get rid of any excess weight sitting on top of those muscles. So if you want a flat stomach, you're going to have to combine those crunches with some type of aerobic exercise, like running, cycling, or swimming. And don't even attempt to get a washboard stomach — most girls and women don't have the muscle mass needed to *ever* get chisled abs and for those who do it's hereditary.

2. **Eating before noon and after eight P.M. will make you fat. False.** It's not *when* you eat, it's *how much* and *what* you eat that determines weight gain. Of course, eating a box of doughnuts just before bed isn't going to do anyone a favor but eating popcorn while watching your favorite shows won't hurt. And avoiding breakfast in the A.M. is a huge mistake. Studies have shown that fueling up in the morning helps you focus and get better grades at school. (Plus, no more embarrassing tummy growls.)

3. **Trimming your hair will make it grow faster. False.** A good diet and regular visits to the hairdresser won't make your hair grow faster but they *will* keep it looking healthy and shiny so there's no harm done there. Hair grows at about a rate of half an inch per month so if you're dying to have long locks by summer, don't get that cute pixie cut to celebrate spring.

4. **If it has "natural" on the label, it's definitely good for you. False.** "Natural" doesn't necessarily mean better for you. Always read the small print to find out how many nutrients and vitamins there are compared to the amounts of fat, sugar, and sodium before you buy into the health-food hard sell.

5. **Cracking your knuckles is bad for your fingers. False.** People used to believe cracking your knuckles would cause arthritis but while it's not a particularly nice habit, doctors say it really won't do you any harm.

6. **If you're wearing sunscreen you can stay in the sun as long as you like. False.** Sunscreen *does* help protect your skin from harmful UVA and UVB rays but don't use it as an excuse to sit and bake in the sun all day. Prolonged exposure to the sun (even with sunscreen on) will definitely still cause skin damage. Plus, you should be reapplying sunscreen every two hours for maximum effectiveness. Now you know.

7. **Bread is bad for you. False.** Unfortunately, carbohydrates like bread and pasta have been getting some bad press lately, but that doesn't mean you shouldn't eat them. According to the nutrition pyramid, carbs should make up the majority of your diet. They're one of the three main food nutrients (along with protein and fat) that are essential for fueling the body. So go ahead — have your bagels and eat your spaghetti, too.

8. **You should use the same brand of shampoo and conditioner. False.** It's totally unnecessary to use the same brand of shampoo and conditioner. That said, you might like the look and smell of your matching hair-care products. Or maybe you've found that one particular brand works best on your hair type. So even though matching your shampoo with your conditioner doesn't particularly help, it can't hurt, either.

9. **Licking your lips helps smooth out the skin. False.** Licking or nibbling your lips might feel good but the results are anything but. When saliva evaporates it actually takes moisture away from your lips, making them even drier and more cracked. Get that smooth feeling with a lip balm instead.

10. Chewing gum can make your teeth crooked. False. If your teeth start to become crooked or are unevenly spaced, it could be due to repeatedly chewing on something hard, like a pencil or pen, but not because of gum. In fact, if you can't brush after lunch, chewing sugarless gum after eating can actually help your teeth by producing saliva, which dissolves sugar and other food particles left on your teeth.

Nail Know-how

Clean, well-kept nails beat dirty, ragged, chewed-on fingers any day. It's as simple as that. Here's how to have 'em:

1. Eat right. For strong, healthy nails, make sure you're eating right. Look for foods high in calcium, zinc, and iron, like leafy greens, rice, red meat, and beans — these nutrients strengthen nails (and bones).

2. One way. When filing your nails, move the emery board in one direction only from the side of the nail to the center. Don't move it back and forth like a saw because that can cause nails to break.

3. **Polish protection.** If you've just started polishing your nails, make sure you apply a base coat of clear polish first to protect nails. You see, dark polish can stain nails yellow if it touches them directly and sparkly polish is a nightmare to remove because it sticks to nails — the layer of clear makes removal easier.

4. **Perfect polish.** When polishing your nails, start with your pinkie finger and work your way up to the thumb — you're less likely to get smudges that way.

5. **Clean up.** If you've smeared polish on your cuticles or fingers, clean up using a Q-Tip dipped in nail polish remover. But wait till your nails are dry first or you'll run the risk of smudging the polish and having to start all over again.

6. Don't bite. If you can't stop nibbling on your nails, keep some cuticle oil or hand cream nearby. Apply the lotion frequently — it'll taste terrible when you chew, plus your hands will be nice and soft!

7. Cuticle care. Don't cut your cuticles or let anyone else do it, either. The cuticle acts as a seal to protect your nails from bacteria and fungus. If you want to keep your cuticles tidy, rub them with moisturizer and then gently push them back with an orange stick (available at any drugstore).

8. Stay strong. If your nails break or chip easily, try polishing them with a nail hardener that you can get at any drugstore. And give your nails a break from regular polish and remover, which can be harsh and dry out nails, making them brittle.

9. Fake faux pas. If you're going to try press-on nails, make sure you take them off within 48 hours and let your nails rest overnight. Dirt and bacteria can get trapped underneath the press-ons, giving you a nasty shock when you take them off.

10. **Tender toes.** Squeezing your feet into tight shoes could result in an ingrown toenail. If one of your toenails becomes red, sore, and swollen, change your shoes and let Mom know immediately. She may be able to help or can take you to the doctor.

Steps to a Great School Photo

Wanting your school photo to come out great doesn't mean you're vain. After all, your friends will probably want to trade wallet photos to keep as mementos and you know this is the shot that Mom will send to every single relative 'round the world. Might as well look your best.

1. **Bright and bold.** Bright, solid colors work better than prints — but you can still wear your favorite plaid shirt as long as it's not too busy. Stay away from white because it'll make you look washed-out.

2. Don't get framed. Glasses tend to cause a reflection in photos, so you might want to take yours off while the photographer's snapping.

3. Don't bare all. Try to avoid sleeveless shirts or low, scoop, or V necks because your skin will look washed-out under bright lights.

4. Keep it simple. You can spend a little more time than usual styling your hair but keep your 'do close to your everyday look. This is a school photo, not Glamour Shots. And you'll want to recognize yourself when the pics come back!

5. Smile. Don't smile just because the photographer makes one of his lame jokes ('cause then it'll look fake). Smile for real because you know it'll make you look prettier, happier, and more relaxed.

6. No chin-up. Don't tilt your head too far back or everyone will get a clear view up your nose!

7. Pearly whites. Brush your teeth before taking your photo. You don't want to get the pics back only to discover a big ole piece of lettuce wedged in your teeth!

8. Once-over. Get a friend to check you out just before you get snapped to make sure everything is zipped, buttoned, and where it should be — and that you don't have any paint on your face from art class.

9. Strike a pose. If the photographer is suggesting a pose or a facial expression you're not comfortable with, don't do it just to make him happy — you'll look your best by acting natural.

10. Open sesame. There's nothing worse than getting a photo back where you look great — all except for the fact that your eyes are closed. To avoid shut eye, ask the photographer to count to three before snapping and then when he gets to two, blink. That way, your eyes'll be back open on three.

Shopping Secrets

Shopping can be a fun and productive experience either as a solo excursion, with a bud, or maybe with Mom. But (a big but!) it can also be a nightmare if there are long checkout lines, a lack of your size clothing, or masses of people in the stores. Following these tips will make your shopping experience easier and better and help you save money — and hopefully you'll build a great wardrobe in the process!

1. Speed is key. Wear easy-to-remove separates while shopping, like a T-shirt and jeans, to make the fitting-room experience easier. This way you'll also be able to try on just tops or bottoms without having to completely undress. Avoid sneakers with tons of laces or a top with a million buttons because they'll slow you down and leave you frustrated.

2. Friendly feedback. Ask a friend to come along while you shop. She can give you valuable feedback — that a shirt you're trying on is totally see-through and should be ditched or that a cute skirt looks great on you and is a keeper.

3. Find a perfect fit. If an item doesn't fit perfectly forget it — because what if you don't grow or gain or lose the weight you need for it to fit? A total waste, that's what.

4. Save money on simple stuff. Try to stick with solid-colored basics that you'll be able to wear for a while and that will match lots of other clothes. If you want to be supertrendy do it with accessories — they are cheaper so you won't feel as bad when they go out of style and you can toss them aside at the end of the season.

5. Don't shop till you drop. Shopping can burn up to 300 calories an hour (all those strenuous outfit changes!) so stop somewhere along the way for a snack before you get grumpy from hunger and start hating everything you see. You'll be back up to speed in no time.

6. Cheaper isn't always better. It's good to be a bargain hunter but don't jump to buy the cheapest version of an item of clothing you find because it may be of inferior quality. If it's not sewn together well, then it'll just fall apart the first time you wash it and you'll end up spending more money to buy a new one! Always carefully check the quality and construction of an item of clothing before you buy it.

7. Shop around. If you are shoe shopping, don't buy the first pair you see. (Or if you're looking for a blue sweater, don't buy the first one that fits.) Check other stores in case they have the same shoes or a sweater on sale. If not, you can always go back.

8. Older is better. The vintage look is huge right now. There's never been a better time to go thrifting (finding cheap, trendy, used stuff) at secondhand stores, the Salvation Army, and antique boutiques. But beware of price mark-ups — since these vintage duds are hot, store owners often jack up the price on very worn-out (sometimes even ripped!) items. Examine them carefully before you lay down your cash.

9. Creature of comfort. If something you try on doesn't feel one hundred percent comfortable, do *not* buy it. If shoes pinch or a shirt is binding or straps dig into your shoulders causing you discomfort while you're trying them on for two minutes, imagine what agony you'll be in after wearing it all day.

10. Think it over. If you see an outrageously expensive dress that you just can't live without, don't decide to buy it right away. Ask the clerk to put it on hold for you. That way you can go home and think it over. If you still want the dress a week later and you think it's worth all that money, you can go back and buy it.

Chapter Six
Earnin' and Learnin'

(**Work It, Girl**)

Cool clothes . . . movie matinees . . . french fries at McDonald's — having fun can break the bank! But alas, you're still too young to get a job at the mall and Mom and Dad aren't buying your inflation argument for needing an allowance increase. Don't despair, with a little entrepreneurial spirit you can find ways to make some extra money. But with all these money-making suggestions be sure to discuss your fee up front so there are no surprises.

1. **Party time.** Got good people skills? Love playing with little kids? Always coming

up with wacky plans for you and your friends? You might make a great party planner. If you baby-sit, talk to the families you baby-sit for, or if you don't, figure out where the little kids in your neighborhood live and speak to their parents. If any of the kids have a birthday coming up, ask their parents if they might want help putting out snacks, organizing games, and ensuring that the kids don't lick the frosting off the birthday cake before the candles are blown out or pin the tail on a kid instead of the donkey. You'd be surprised how many parents would welcome the extra help. You can charge more than the usual baby-sitting rate because there are more kids involved.

2. **Girl Friday.** Most adults have a million and one things to do every day so you might be able to help lighten their load and make some money in the process. Let Mom, Dad, and their friends know that for a small fee you're willing to run their errands or do other chores, like making a trip to the post office or the library to return their overdue books, or folding their laundry!

3. **Smart cookie.** Are you a math whiz or do you play a mean guitar? Your talents could land you a job as a tutor. Put flyers up around your neighborhood (the library, town recreation center, and local church info center are good places) letting parents know what your areas of expertise are. You never know, you may get a call from parents who are willing to hire you to teach Johnny or Jane how to solve those multiplication problems.

4. **A pet's best friend.** Let your neighbors know that you've got a way with animals. You could offer to walk, wash, or even just play with their pets when they're too busy or away. You get to bond with Buster and get paid, too!

5. **Nature girl.** No matter what the season, there are always yard chores to be done. You can offer to cut grass in the summer, rake leaves in the fall, shovel snow in the winter, and plant flowers in the spring. You'll be a year-round money-making machine!

6. **Daily news.** Local newspapers are always looking for kids to deliver around the neighborhood. If you don't mind a little hard work (lugging the weekend edition is a killer) or some early rising (routes start before daybreak), the tips are good. But check with Mom and Dad first because they might not be crazy about you getting up before the crack of dawn or being outside before it's totally light out. (They might agree to help out by driving you on your route.)

7. High-tech consultant. Are your parents always coming to you for help with their PC? You can turn your computer skills into a business by troubleshooting for those folks with technical difficulties. You can get paid to install software and create Web pages for the adults around you who just don't get it.

8. Salesgirl. You might not be able to join the workforce just yet but don't let that stop you from becoming a top-notch salesgirl. Let neighbors know that you're willing to organize and run their weekend garage sales — for a small profit, of course.

9. Lather up. All you need is a bucket and some sponges and you can car wash your way to making enough dough for at least a movie and snacks. Let neighbors know you are willing to make their cars shine for a small fee. You might not be able to rely on this money-making method during the winter but during the summer you'll have a blast earning cash.

10. **Home alone.** Your clients can vacation worry-free, knowing that you're looking after things back at home. Snagging a job as a house-sitter means checking the mailbox and picking up the newspaper every day so it looks like someone's home, watering plants, and just making sure that there are no major problems.

P.S. Before taking any of these jobs, check with the folks first and NEVER offer your services to strangers. Got it?

Baby-sitting 101

It sounded like a good idea at the time — make some money while playing with some adorable munchkins. But now the folks are gone and those cute kids have turned into screaming monsters and you don't know what to do. Help! Brush up on your baby-sitting skills so you can handle any situation and continue to sit in the future.

1. **Get smart.** If you're lacking in the child-care-experience department, try taking a class with a local chapter of a reputable organization like the Red Cross, the YMCA or YWCA, or the Girl Scouts. You'll learn what to do in any situation, from changing a diaper to performing CPR.

2. **Go with those you know.** If you're looking for some baby-sitting gigs, try asking friends, family, and teachers for possible contacts. You can even try your immediate neighbors. But don't, under any circumstances, accept an offer from a stranger (even if it's the new family that moved in down the street) or anyone who makes you uncomfortable.

3. **Have a plan.** Always let your parents know where you're going to be (make sure they have the phone number and address) and how long you expect to be there — you can always call home with an update if your plans change. If the family you're baby-sitting for can't take you home, make sure your parents know that you need to be picked up.

4. House rules. Have the parents establish the house rules before they leave — preferably in front of the kids so everyone's clear on what is (and more important, what isn't) allowed. Ask questions about everything from which snacks and TV shows are okay, to any allergies the kids have, to bedtimes. Knowing this stuff in advance will save you the hassle of having to track down the parents while they're out.

5. Money can be funny. Before beginning to baby-sit, ask friends who already do what the going rate is. Also keep in mind that more kids mean more money and then be sure to agree on an hourly rate with the parents before you start the job.

6. Get the 411. Have the parents show you where important items, like the phone and the medicine cabinet, are so that you can find them quickly in an emergency. Before they leave, make sure you get the phone number of where they will be that evening (plus their cell phone number if they have one). It's also a good idea to have a neighbor's number in case you need to get a hold of someone nearby.

7. **Follow (most of) the rules.** A baby-sitter is a bit like a substitute teacher — never as strict as the regular teacher. The kids should still brush their teeth, bathe before going to bed, and do all the important stuff, but maybe you can let them stay up half an hour longer or allow them to have an extra cookie as a treat. But just 'cause Mom and Dad aren't there doesn't mean all the rules should be broken.

8. **Be prepared.** Some parents will have your whole evening planned, complete with popcorn, snacks, and a bunch of Blockbuster movies. But you might not always be so lucky. The kids might have some cool toys but bringing some fun games and ideas for craft projects of your own is never a bad idea. A baby-sitter who puts some effort into making the kids happy will likely be asked back.

9. **Keep it clean.** Run through a mental checklist after the kids go to bed. Have you locked all the doors and turned off unnecessary lights? Did you clean up any mess the kids might have made? The parents might not pay you any extra for your effort but they will appreciate your thoughtfulness and call you again in the future.

10. **Play it safe.** If you run into a problem and you're not one hundred percent sure you can handle it, don't be afraid to call the kids' parents, your own parents, or a neighbor for help. The biggest mistake you can make is doing nothing.

Baby-sitting Supplies

Stock your baby-sitting bag with these essentials that will make the whole baby-sitting endeavor go more smoothly.

1. **A well-stocked first-aid kit.** In case you can't find theirs fast enough or if theirs is missing something you need.

2. Construction paper. For coloring and crafts.

3. Craft scissors. Also for crafts.

4. Yarn, buttons, and beads. Yup, you got it — for crafts, yet again. If any of the kids you're baby-sitting are under three, be careful — they could easily swallow or choke on buttons and beads.

5. Washable markers and crayons. For drawing and coloring.

6. Playing cards. Great for kids who are slightly older.

7. Storybooks. Kids love to be read to (even the ones who already know how to read themselves) and listening to a story often lulls 'em to sleep (extra bonus!).

8. Tapes and CDs. Raffi, Barney, or the sound track to Disney's latest animated flick can keep 'em enthralled for hours. And the singing and dancing will tire them out.

9. **Old clothes, funny hats, and shoes.** To play dress-up.

10. **Videos.** Pop in a tape of the latest blockbuster kids' movie to hit the video store shelves and the kids will love you. Tapes of popular TV shows are another good bet.

(Get Smart)

Doing well in school has a lot to do with how much hard-core studying and effort you're willing to do. Luckily there are a few other methods you can try to give you an extra edge.

1. **Drink water.** You need about eight glasses of water a day to stay hydrated — if you run low you could get tired and have a hard time focusing. Since seventy-five percent of the brain is made up of H_2O, it's in your best interest to chug lots of the stuff.

2. **Eat breakfast.** Never mind that Mom says it's the most important meal of the day — you can't ignore the facts: According to the American Dietetic Association, kids who start the school day fueled up on a full stomach get higher test scores and are able to concentrate better. Can't argue with data like that!

3. Take your vitamins. Vitamins C (found in citrus fruits and green leafy veggies) and E (found in nuts and eggs) get rid of debris in your body called free radicals, which can damage brain cells. By eating foods high in these and other important vitamins or through vitamin supplements, you can improve your memory, judgment, perception, and reasoning.

4. Keep a journal. Don't bottle up your problems and anxiety — what a total waste of brain space! Write your thoughts and feelings down to get them out. Then later you can look at them with a fresh perspective and might get some insight into what's bothering you and why — then you'll be able to move on to concentrate on more important things.

5. Shut-eye. Avoid a major cramming session just before a test. According to recent studies, getting a good night's sleep before a test can help you do well, while getting too little sleep will just leave you bleary-eyed and unable to concentrate the next day. It's always best to get studying or other schoolwork done ahead of time. Sleep tight.

6. Fish food. Eat your tuna and salmon. Turns out these fish contain Omega-3 fatty acids — it may sound gross but these actually stimulate "alert" chemicals in your brain, helping you concentrate and stay focused.

7. Music for the mind. While the results are only temporary (bummer), studies show that listening to classical music (Mozart, Bach, Beethoven) while studying results in achieving higher test scores. Knowing how to read and play music also makes you smarter — overall, kids who play instruments score higher in abstract reasoning tests.

8. Flower power. Some scents, like vanilla, are meant for relaxation, while others have the opposite effect and can improve alertness. A mixed floral scent speeds up the learning process.

9. **Stimulate your mind.** Expose yourself to new experiences and you'll be forcing your brain to learn how to adapt to new surroundings. This type of mental workout will pay off when you sit down to a pop quiz that came from nowhere.

10. **Play ball.** The focus and dedication you apply during gym class will pay off in test scores. Female athletes, who are already used to hard work, strategizing, and discipline, tend to perform better academically.

Make the World a Better Place

Want to make a difference? Let the following do-good list of ideas inspire you to leave your mark on — if not the world — your neighborhood, at least.

1. **The three Rs.** Reduce, reuse, and recycle as much stuff as you can, including glass, plastic, aluminum, and paper products. If you've got a garden and your parents are willing, suggest creating a compost heap made up of your biodegradable trash — any gardening book can tell you how. Compost is a great fertilizer — your flowers will thank you for it.

2. Go veggie. Try becoming a vegetarian or at least eating less meat. Save a cow and stop the expansion of grazing fields.

3. Child's play. Make sure today's kids grow up to be tomorrow's leaders. Lead story time at the local library or volunteer at an after-school program at the local community center. Extra one-on-one attention is often a big deal and can make a difference to a needy kid (or even a not-so-needy one).

4. Litterbug. Throw every wrapper, scrap of paper, and wad of gum away. Don't treat the world like your own personal garbage can.

5. Cyber charity. At a loss for what to do or how to get started? Check out *www.dosomething.org* and *www.impactonline.org*. These Web sites match volunteers with non-profit organizations in their communities. The Do Something Web site also helps do-gooders set up their own charities.

6. The great outdoors. Check your newspaper's local listings for beach, park, and forest cleanups you can participate in. You can also get involved with an environmental group like Greenpeace. Contact Greenpeace at 800-326-0959 or *www.greenpeaceusa.org*.

7. Feed someone. Hold a food drive in your neighborhood, classroom, or local grocery store to help out needy families. Collect cans and other nonperishable items, then donate them to a local food bank or community center, or contact an organization like Second Harvest (800-532-FOOD or *www.secondharvest.org*) that will distribute them to the needy.

8. Just do it. Ask your guidance counselor what charitable clubs exist at your school and join one. If none do, create one.

9. Neighborhood watch. Practice random acts of kindness in your neighborhood: Ask a senior citizen if you could help out by running errands, pick up an overturned trash can, or deliver flowers from your garden without anyone having to ask and without expecting anything in return.

10. **Respect yourself.** Fight for what you believe in, even if it's not the most popular choice: That might mean speaking up in class if you feel the teacher is discriminating against someone or telling your friends they're making a mistake when they throw their plastic burger wrappers on the ground. It might not make you more popular but at least you'll be able to live with yourself.

Ace This Year

School doesn't have to be a dark cloud following you everywhere you go. Don't sweat it. Hard work, strategic seating, and careful planning can help you boost your grades and ace this school year.

1. **Pick the right seat.** If you're allowed to choose where you sit in class, then where you park it ends up saying a lot about your attitude. Sitting in the back row might suggest you're trying not to be noticed and are not into class — instead aim for somewhere in the front or middle of the class. If your teacher assigns seats and you end up way in the back, ask if you can switch to the front or middle.

2. Please the prof. Always get to know your teachers. Take notes, ask questions, and hand in your assignments on time. Teachers can be pretty subjective, so making a good impression could swing your grade from a B+ to an A−.

3. The write stuff. Learn how to take good notes so you'll have all the material you need to study before a test. Pay special attention if a teacher slows down and speaks loudly, repeats material, or writes anything on the board. Chances are this material will make its way into the test.

4. Speak up in class. If you don't understand something, make a habit of asking questions right away. Class participation can score you major points — at the very least the teacher will be sure to remember your name. If speaking up in front of all your classmates gives you nightmares, stay after class to talk to your teacher.

5. **Clean up clutter.** Keep your locker, desk, and backpack organized. The stress of a mess will interfere with your studying. So spend a couple of minutes every day clearing up your study space and getting rid of scraps of paper, old lunches, and notes you no longer need. Then you can totally concentrate on the studying at hand.

6. **Study schedule.** Study hardest for a test at least two nights before the exam actually is to take place. That way you can get a good night's rest the evening before your exam. It's the best way for your brain to process all the information you've taken in and more likely to result in a high test score.

7. **Sit alone.** When you're walking into an exam, don't make a beeline for your friends. It's not about being antisocial, but the time before a test should be a time for you to focus on the task at hand — namely, acing the test! You don't want to end up having a major debate with your friends about whether you were supposed to study chapter four for the test — that'll only stress you out and could affect your test performance.

8. Do not disturb. You might want to aim to sit in the middle of the class during regular classes, but during an exam try to sit at the back, if possible. That way there's no one tapping you on the shoulder asking to borrow a pencil or kicking your chair. Try not to look at others during the exam to avoid the stress of seeing someone finish their exam while you're only halfway through.

9. Follow directions. Read the directions carefully so you don't lose points on something as silly as putting your name in the wrong spot. If you are running out of time, at least make sure you complete the section that counts for the most points.

10. Move on. Don't beat yourself up over a bad grade, just see how you can do better. Ask the teacher for extra tutoring; it shows you're interested in improving.

The Coolest Web Sites

Music, shopping, great advice, and new friends — the Web's sort of like your room, the mall, and school all rolled into one. It's the best. Just make sure you're not neglecting school and real friends while you roam around cyberspace. And *never ever* give out any personal info to any person or company you encounter on the Web.

1. **www.celebritysightings.com** Find the official fan club Web sites of all your favorite stars, plus you can chat with supercool celebs and play fun games.

2. **www.mtv.com** It's sort of like watching MTV on the tube — you'll get reviews, news, concert info, buzz clips, and celebrity chats, plus the scoop on all of MTV's cool shows.

3. **www.gurl.com** All-around great site for girls. Includes advice, fiction, interesting news bits and info, reviews of books and movies, plus tons of links to other great sites. Plus, the site is affiliated with Delia's so you

can also check out their latest stuff and even make purchases right on-line.

4. **www.planetgirl.com** Quizzes, games, cyber pals, true-life stories, and techie advice all brought to you by Girlgames, producers of CD-ROM games for girls.

5. **www.phys.com** Rate your health habits, get nutrition and fitness advice, and find info on every sport you've ever been curious to try.

6. **www.homeworkheaven.com** With this on-line encyclopedia, you can find all kinds of info on subjects like math, geography, science, government, languages, history, and more. You can also use the search engine to look for a keyword or get help from an on-site expert.

7. **www.sonicnet.com** Get the latest music news, juicy gossip, album reviews, and hot videos 24/7. Plus you can log on to live cyber chats with some of your favorite musical artists.

8. **www.zeeks.com** This colorful site for kids offers cool stuff like free e-mail, chat rooms, tons of games, funny polls to answer, and lots of great trivia. Plus there's great personal advice and techie tips for cyber-savvy girls.

9. **www.mrshowbiz.com** Got a crush on a Hollywood hottie? Want to find out more about your fave actress, TV show, or band? Mr. Showbiz has the scoop on actors, musicians, sports stars, and the latest flicks. You'll find bios, celebrity gossip, and a list of recent interviews with favorite superstars, and more.

10. **www.onnow.com** This site has an up-to-date list of tons of chats and on-line events happening all over the Web. Find out where and when to tune in for the latest sports, celebrity, movie, and music events.

Conclusion
Top Tens Forever

Most of the advice you've read here is just plain common sense — the kind of suggestions that might make you say, "Why didn't I think of that?" But it's hard to be an expert at handling your own life, especially when you're caught up in a fight with your best friend or trying to finish a huge report for school.

The next time you're confronted with a situation you're not sure how to handle, step back and take a moment. Every problem has a solution, you just have to find it. Search within yourself, explore your options, talk to family and friends — and hopefully you *will* find the answers you need.